H[enry] Clay Trumbull

The captured scout of the army of the James

A sketch of the life of sergeant Henry H. Manning

H[enry] Clay Trumbull

The captured scout of the army of the James
A sketch of the life of sergeant Henry H. Manning

ISBN/EAN: 9783742844088

Manufactured in Europe, USA, Canada, Australia, Japa

Cover: Foto ©Thomas Meinert / pixelio.de

Manufactured and distributed by brebook publishing software
(www.brebook.com)

H[enry] Clay Trumbull

The captured scout of the army of the James

THE

CAPTURED SCOUT

OF THE

ARMY OF THE JAMES.

A Sketch of the Life of

SERGEANT HENRY H. MANNING,

OF THE TWENTY-FOURTH MASS. REGIMENT.

BY

CHAPLAIN H. CLAY TRUMBULL.

BOSTON:
NICHOLS AND NOYES.
1869.

CAMBRIDGE:

PRESS OF JOHN WILSON AND SON.

TO THE SURVIVING MEMBERS

OF THE

Twenty-Fourth Regiment Massachusetts Vols.,

THIS SKETCH OF THEIR COMRADE IS AFFECTIONATELY

DEDICATED,

BY ONE WHO HOLDS IN EVER FRESH AND DELIGHTFUL

REMEMBRANCE HIS THREE YEARS' EXPERIENCE

AS THEIR BRIGADE COMPANION,

AND

HIS MINISTRY AS THEIR OCCASIONAL CHAPLAIN.

NOTE.

THIS little sketch is the best, because the only, tribute to the memory of its subject that the writer, amid the pressure of varied duties, can find time to render.

Prepared, in great part, for use in a memorial discourse, it has not been rewritten, although extended by additions which perhaps mar the harmony of its first design.

The fact that it was shaped to be spoken rather than to be read, — designed for the ear rather than for the eye, — will account, to those accustomed to public address, for some of its unsuitableness of style for the form in which it now appears.

H. C. T.

CONTENTS.

THE CAPTURED SCOUT

OF THE

ARMY OF THE JAMES.

THE DEAD OF THE ARMY OF THE JAMES.

ON the evening of Wednesday, Sept. 2, 1868, some two hundred ex-officers of the "Army of the James" were assembled in the dining-hall of the St. James Hotel, Boston, in delightful re-union, as comrades of camp and campaigning. The writer of this little sketch was called on to say words in tribute to "The memory of the honored dead" of that army, and in consequence the tenderest recollections were revived of those who fell in the long years of war with rebellion.

Hardly had the writer reached his home from that re-union, before word came to him of the

death of another soldier of the Army of the
James; one whose varied and thrilling experi-
ences, peculiar services to the Union cause, and
noble Christian character entitled him to special
mention, as a noteworthy and satisfactory illus-
tration of the bravery and worth of the enlisted
men of that army. While on his death-bed, this
young soldier had sent particular request to one
who, as an army chaplain in his brigade, had
known something of his personal character and
history, to preach a commemorative discourse
on the occasion of his decease. Thus called on
again to pay just tribute to the memory of the
dead of the Army of the James, the writer prepared this sketch as part of a sermon preached
at Warwick, Mass., Sept. 13, 1868, and now
gives it to the public at the request of those who,
knowing something of the young soldier's history, naturally desire to know more.

COST OF THE SLAVEHOLDERS' WAR.

Others than his immediate comrades have
reasons for an interest in this young soldier,
and should join in honoring his memory, and

recalling at his death the record of his army life. Dying though he did among the green hills of Massachusetts, in these days of palmy peace, with parents and sisters ministering to his comfort, as he wasted slowly before their loving gaze, he was really one of the dead of the war, one of the starved of Andersonville. His vigorous constitution was broken down under the malarial damps of the sea-island death-swamps, beneath the smiting sun-glare of the Carolina sands, in the fatigues of dreary marches and anxious picket service, and amid the excitements of battle and the crushing responsibilities of a mission of imminent peril within the lines of the enemy. His young life was really worn away, not here at the North, but there at the South, in dragging months of imprisonment, in teeming hours of attempted escape, in rapid flight from the swift pursuers, and in the death-clutch with the fierce-fanged hounds in the swamp of despair!

And he was but one of many, — a representative youth ; one out of thirteen thousand martyrs of Andersonville, —

> "The men who perished in swamp and fen,
> The slowly starved of the prison pen;"—

a solitary soldier among fully three hundred
thousand who gave their lives for the nation's
life, the sodden mounds of whose graves, like an
encircling earthwork, make secure that nation's
proud though dearly-bought position among the
kingdoms of the world. Surely, there is little
danger that the story of such a man will be told
too widely, or his services be too highly esteemed;
small cause for fear, that, in the glad days of rest
from war, there will be too vividly recalled those
dark hours of the imperilled republic, when the
bared right arms of two and a half millions of
loyal and loving Union soldiers and sailors were
essential to the preservation of a free and righteous government; and not only each blood-drop
shed by those who stood or fell in battle for their
country, but every heart-throb of their suffering
or toil, and every tear of those who loved them,
counted on the ransom of Liberty, and helped—

> "To make, for children yet to come,
> This land of their bequeathing,
> The imperial and the peerless home
> Of happiest beings breathing."

A MASSACHUSETTS BOY.— FORESHADOW-INGS OF A NOBLE LIFE.

Henry Hatch Manning was born in Warwick, Mass., May 17, 1844. He was ever a loving and dutiful son and brother. Just before his death, his mother remarked, " I cannot now recall any act of his disobedience."—" Our brightest earthly hopes will perish with him," added his sister. When young, his frequent wish was that he had been the eldest child, so as to lift burdens his sisters now must bear. At eight years old, he was at work for a neighbor, earning something beyond his board. While thus occupied, he was startled by the sudden death of his employer by accident. Hurrying to his home, he whispered the sad story to his mother, adding in almost the same breath, " But don't tell father. He wouldn't let me go back; and what would Mrs. Holmes do without me?" Thus early he showed his independence of character, and his desire to live for others.

Having the ordinary common-school advantages of a Massachusetts town,— such as are now,

thank God ! extended into regions whither they
won an entrance by blood, — Henry Manning im-
proved them well. He had, moreover, faithful
home instruction ; and the influence of a Christian
mother's prayerful teachings followed him like
a continual benediction. When about sixteen
years old, while at work in another town from
this, in a season of spiritual declension and cold-
ness there, he was drawn by God's Spirit to make
a full surrender of himself to Jesus. Evil influences were around him just then : a sneering
scoffer sought persistently to dissuade him from
his new-formed purpose ; but God was with him,
and he witnessed faithfully for Christ. Others
followed his example, and a precious revival of
God's Spirit-work followed in that long cold and
formal community.

THE SOLDIER OF CHRIST AND COUNTRY.

It was soon after this that the echo of rebel
guns against Fort Sumter aroused the New-
England sons of Revolutionary patriots to the
perils of the nationality their fathers had founded
in blood. Henry Manning was not yet seven-

teen when the old flag was dishonored in Charleston-Harbor; but he was old enough to realize his country's need, and patriotic enough to stake every thing in her defence. His heart, warm with new love for the Saviour who died for him, throbbed to evidence its affection in some sacrifice for a cause approved of God. Delayed somewhat in his original plans, he enlisted, in the early autumn of 1861, as a private in the Twenty-fourth Massachusetts Regiment, then forming near Boston, under the gallant and lamented Stevenson.

After his enlistment, on the Sabbath before he left for the war, he stood up alone in his home-church, and made public profession of his new faith, and was there enrolled as a follower of Jesus; his pastor preaching an appropriate sermon from the text, " Thou therefore endure hardness, as a good soldier of Jesus Christ ;" which inspired counsel Manning certainly followed to the letter. Going out thence, clad·in the " whole armor of God," Manning commenced his career· as a soldier of the cross and his country, and thenceforward followed unflinchingly the flag of

his government and the blood-stained banner of
Jesus.

A GOOD REGIMENT. — A GOOD RECORD.

The Twenty-fourth Massachusetts was a noble
battalion, with a glorious record. Through its
four years of service, its well-earned reputation
for good discipline, thorough drill, and stanch
courage was unsurpassed; and few regiments
were its equals in hard fighting and practical
efficiency. It would be enough for any man's
soldierly reputation that he stood well in that
regiment; for he who won honor there deserved
it everywhere. Hence the good name there
secured by Henry Manning shows his personal worth, and indicates the value of his
services. Said Col. Ordway, at the close of
Manning's term of service, "I have known his
whole course since he has been a soldier. . . .
He has always been a brave, faithful, truthful,
soldier, . . . honest and temperate, and in every
way to be trusted." Maj. Edmands added, "I
can cheerfully say, that I have never known a
braver man in the regiment — and I was formerly

his captain. He is, I believe, competent to fill any position where fidelity, integrity, and energy are required." Adjutant Stoddard also testified, "[He] has always been especially noticed for the efficient manner in which he has performed his duties as a soldier: always ready for any daring undertaking, he has won for himself a place in the hearts of the officers and his comrades of the Twenty-fourth Massachusetts; and his name can never be obliterated from the pages of the history of that regiment."

FIGHTING AND PRAYING.

The Twenty-fourth went out in the Burnside expedition to the waters of North Carolina, and, passing the perils of Hatteras " Swash," had an honorable and distinguished part, under brave and beloved Gen. John G. Foster, in the battles of Roanoke, Newbern, Little Washington, Rawl's Mills, Kinston, Whitehall, and Goldsboro'. In all this service, Manning gained in manliness and in the Christian graces, under the developing influences of active army life. At Kinston he had a narrow escape from death. A bullet

struck the rail of a fence, behind which he was
stationed as a sharpshooter, just in range of his
head ; a knot turned it aside so that it barely
passed his cheek, scattering the splinters in his
eyes.

In the spring and early summer of 1863, the
Twenty-fourth was in South Carolina, passing
months on the sickly sea-islands, where it was said
no white man had before lived at that season of
the year. It was there that the writer of this
sketch — then chaplain of another regiment in the
same brigade — first met young Manning. His
regiment then having no chaplain, he was one of
an association of earnest Christians who had
banded together to keep up religious meetings,
and to do good as they had opportunity, among
their fellows. Under their rustic canopy of
boughs, beneath the grand old live oaks, and
amid the stately palms of Seabrook Island, were
enjoyed never-to-be-forgotten hours of prayer
and praise.

JAMES ISLAND. — HOSPITAL SUPPLY OF REBEL SHELLS.

From Seabrook to James Island, the Twenty-fourth moved, in July, 1863, under Gen. Terry, in co-operation with Gen. Gillmore's advance on Morris Island. Stricken down with sun-stroke there, his whole system prostrate under repeated attacks of fever and chills, fastened on him in the malarial regions of his recent service, Manning lay sick in the rude regimental hospital on the morning of July 16, when the enemy in force made a sudden attack on the Union lines. The shock of this battle was bravely met by Col. Shaw's Fifty-fourth Massachusetts regiment, then first in action. The hospital of the Twenty-fourth was found to be in the focus of the enemy's sharpest fire, and a hurried move was ordered down the island. As the poor invalids, with failing limbs, dragged their tedious way to the beach, shell after shell from the enemy's guns came shrieking past, or bursting among them. One such seemed to explode in Manning's very face, and he fell, with the half

conviction that it had killed him. As he rose
again to his feet, another burst above him, and a
ragged fragment of the hot iron tore down along
his very side, laying open his clothing, and bruis-
ing and lacerating his arm. But this injury prob-
ably saved him from a severer; for, checked by
it a moment, he saw yet another shell explode
directly before him, in the group he had fallen
behind, killing and wounding not a few of that
number. Sorry comfort, this, for sick soldiers!
Yet such was but an incident in the trying army
service of our Union soldiers, in the prolonged
war with rebellion.

CHARLESTON SIEGE-WORK. — SHARP-SHOOTING.

Immediately after the fight at James Island,
the Twenty-fourth passed over to Morris Island,
to have a part in the operations against Charles-
ton from that point, commencing with that terrible
assault on Fort Wagner in which Col. Shaw lost
his life,—when Gen. Stevenson's brigade (includ-
ing the Twenty-fourth) was in reserve, holding
the front after the sad repulse. There, Manning

was again stricken down with sunstroke. Later, he was assigned to a company of sharpshooters in active service at the extreme front. He then had narrow escapes daily. On one occasion, as he and a comrade were alternating in rifle firing through a loop-hole, he had thrown himself down to rest under his rubber blanket, raised for a shade, when a bullet wounded his comrade in the face; as he sprang up to aid him, a huge fragment of a mortar shell came tearing down through the air, and. crushed the rubber blanket into the ground on the very spot where Manning had lain. Those were toilsome days on Morris Island, in the slow dragging siege; men who were there will not soon forget its shifting sands, its blazing sunlight, its unintermitted fire of artillery and musketry, its labors on traverse and parallel and sap, its frequent struggles of sortie or assault, and its atmosphere laden with disease:

"How they marched together, sound or sick,
　Sank in the trench o'er the heavy spade!
How they charged on the guns at double-quick,
Kept ranks for Death to choose and to pick,
　And lay on the beds no fair hands made!"

The Twenty-fourth sweltered and toiled with
the other regiments, and won for itself a proud
name by its brilliant charge on the rifle-pits in the
very face of Wagner's guns. Thence it passed
down the coast to Florida, and had a little rest in
the quaint old Spanish city of St. Augustine.

VETERAN RE-ENLISTMENTS. — LOVE FOR THE OLD FLAG.

It was while the regiment was at St. Augustine that the call came from the government for
the re-enlistment of its veteran soldiers. It did
not take Henry Manning much longer to make
up his mind to a second enlistment than it did
to the first. Had he been wanted for thirty or
fifty years, instead of three or five, he would
doubtless have been ready. God be praised that
such boys lived, and were willing to die, in the
hour of our country's need!

A little incident, occurring as the veterans of
the Twenty-fourth left St. Augustine, on the furlough granted them as a consideration of re-enlistment, well illustrated the character and spirit of
the soldiers of the war. They were gathered

about the head of the dock, just ready to embark
for the North, to leave soldier-life for a while
behind them. Their thoughts were naturally of
their release from service, and of the homes and
loved ones to which they were hastening. Their
comrades, who were to remain behind, had assembled to see them off: citizens of the old town
were also there; and all was glad-hearted cheer-
fulness. But unexpectedly to nearly all, as they
stood thus together, the regimental colors were
brought down from Fort Marion, to be taken
with them to the North. As the dear old flag
came in sight, — the bullet-rent and storm-worn
colors which they had followed unflinchingly on
the weary march and in the battle's crash, and
for which so many whom they loved had died, —
instinctively, as by the word of command, every
voice was hushed; every farewell stayed; and
the soldier group parted and fell back on either
hand, in reverent, affectionate regard for that
symbol of all that they lived for then; and, as
through the open ranks the loved flag was borne
down the pier to the steamer's deck, —

> "Every foot was quiet,
> Every head was bare;
> The soft trade-wind was lifting
> A hundred locks of hair;"

while tearful eyes, in bronzed and manly faces bore precious testimony to the patriotism and generous, devotion of those brave and tender-hearted soldiers. It was with such men and in that spirit that Henry Manning came home, in the spring of 1864, on his veteran furlough.

CAMPAIGNS IT IN VIRGINIA.—VOLUNTEERS AS A SCOUT.

Rejoining his regiment at Gloucester Point, Va., he was in Gen. Butler's expedition up the James River, towards Drewry's Bluff. Early in June, while the Army of the James was shut in the peninsula at Bermuda Hundred, Gen. Butler called for a volunteer scout — or quasi spy — to venture within the enemy's lines, and bring back information of his position and numbers. This call found a ready response in Manning's heart, and he volunteered for the undertaking. He found, as he said in writing to his. home of his determination, peculiar satisfaction in the thought that he could now be of real service to the cause he loved. On the vedette-post, in the rifle-pit, or on the battle-line, he must stand or fall as one man, doing only what any lad might compass; but in this new mission, all his nervous energy and cautious shrewdness and consecrated purpose would tell in an effort worthy of a soldier, whether that effort brought success or failure. As expressive of his feelings, he enclosed to his friends the following lines he had clipped from some paper : —

"We must forget all feelings save the *one;*
We must resign all passions save our purpose;
We must behold no object save OUR COUNTRY,
And only look on death as beautiful,
So that the sacrifice ascend to heaven
And draw down freedom on her evermore."

It requires not a little moral courage and true nerve to deliberately leave one's military lines in the face of the enemy, and pass over into the encircling forces of the foe. But Henry Manning had counted the cost of his undertaking; and late on the evening of June 7, 1864, he glided stealthily down the steep right bank of the river

James, and along the water's edge in the shade
of the heavy foliage, until he had passed the
rebel picket in front of the famous "Howlett
Battery;" then cautiously, and with bated
breath, he crept up the bank, and was within
the enemy's intrenchments. Bayonets glistened,
lights flashed, voices hummed about him: he
was everywhere surrounded by sights and sounds
of life, but he saw never a friendly look, heard
never a friendly note.

> "He hears the rustling flag,
>   And the armed sentry's tramp;
> And the starlight and moonlight
>   His silent wanderings lamp.
>
> With slow tread and still tread,
>   He scans the tented line;
> And he counts the battery guns
>   By the gaunt and shadowy pine;
> And his slow tread and still tread
>   Give no warning sound."

Carefully making his observations, he passed
from point to point up and down the intrench-
ment lines, out to the Richmond pike, and beyond to the Petersburg railroad. Concealing
himself during the day, he scouted again on the
second night. The defences of the enemy were

noted, with the general disposition and number of the troops. Long after this he wrote, " [I was] in possession of such valuable information that if I could only have got back with it, all the time, treasure, and blood which have been spent before Petersburg would have been spared. It could have been captured then with very small loss." But the attempt to regain the Union lines must be postponed until the following night, now that the dawn of the second day found him far from his starting point; so, seeking a secluded spot in the forest, near Chester Station, he concealed himself in its cover, and was soon fast asleep.

THE CAPTURE.—THE DUNGEON.—THE GALLOWS.

Awaking after a few hours, he heard the unexpected murmur of voices near him. A change of position had been made by some of the troops, and he was surrounded by the enemy. He hardly moved before he was discovered.

> " A sharp clang, a steel clang!
> And terror in the sound;
> For the sentry, falcon-eyed,
> In the camp a spy hath found:
> With a sharp clang, a steel clang,
> The patriot is bound."

As a prisoner he was hurried before Brig.-
Gen. Johnson, and by him sent forward to Gen.
Beauregard's headquarters. The order to him
from Gen. Butler, being found on his person,
gave color to the charge that he was an authorized spy; and the first proposition was to hang
him at once to a tree. Indeed, he was told that
his body should swing before sundown. But
from some reason it was decided to try him by
formal court-martial ; and he was sent to Petersburg, where he was shut in a vile hole, under-
neath the jail, " a low, filthy dungeon," as he
described it, "dark, gloomy, and crawling with
vermin." Those who have never been prison-
ers of war under special charges, in the gloom of
solitary confinement, with the staring gallows
threatened, cannot fully realize the terribleness
of Henry Manning's struggle of mind during that
first night in the Petersburg dungeon. Earnestly

did he call on God for strength, that, if he must yield his young life thus and then, he might be faithful even unto such a death. And God sustained him.

GLOOM OF THE STOCKADE AND JAIL.

"I will lift up mine eyes to the hills."

Manning was sent to Georgia for trial. By mistake he was carried with a party to Andersonville, and turned into that place of yet untold horrors; but thither, after seven days, he was tracked out by the authorities, and to them turned over by the brutal Capt. Wirz, who, at parting, shook his clenched fist in his face, and cursed him vehemently as "one of Butler's spies," disgracing that foul stockade by his temporary presence. Thence to Macon, he was shut in a felon's cell in the common jail. There the days dragged heavily, while he lacked air, exercise, fitting food, hope. He pined away until it seemed as if he could not live. "I heard it whispered around, many a time," he wrote afterwards, "'Poor Manning! What a pity that he

must die in such a place as this. Poor boy! he's
past recovery.'" It was while shut in there, an-
ticipating trial, conviction, death, that Manning
cast himself before the Lord, and cried mightily
for help. On his knees, behind the grated door
of his hope-barred cell, he pleaded that he might
yet have life and again find liberty. Although
in intense and agonized earnestness, he yet
prayed in trustful submission to God's righteous
will; and, in no mere selfish love of ease and
safety, solemnly he promised there that if his life
was spared, it should be given wholly and heart-
ily to the service of Jesus. In relating this incident after his release, he added artlessly, "I told
God that if my life was spared, I should know
He did it, for there was no other hope for me,
then." That prayer and that vow seemed to be
favorably heard of God. An alarm from an an-
ticipated attack startled the authorities at Macon;
the provost-marshal of the post was ordered on
active duty; in the transfer of authorities, the
charges against Manning were lost, and in consequence his court-martial trial did not take
place. But his personal trials were by no means

at an end. His tedious prison-life had barely
commenced.

ESCAPE AND RECAPTURE.—TORN BY BLOOD-HOUNDS.

With some of his fellow-prisoners he made
several attempts at escape : once he was actually
outside the jail, but was soon retaken. From the
jail he was removed to the Macon stockade.
Digging out thence, he was making his way
towards our lines at Atlanta,—travelling only
nights, resting in the woods by day,—when he
was caught by a rebel scout, and returned to his
prison quarters. From Macon he was taken to
Millen, to be guarded in the stockade at Camp
Lawton. Returned to Macon, he was ordered
thence again to Andersonville. Shrinking from
the horrors of that well-remembered pen, he was
willing to risk every thing in another attempt at
escape on his way thither. Going by rail, he
determined to jump from the moving train ; and,
as several who had thus jumped with the cars in
slow motion had been shot down by the guard,
he made up his mind to leap while the train was

at highest speed. On a down grade, he made
the fearful plunge, and, as though by a miracle,
he rolled unharmed down the embankment and
into the ditch below. Quick as thought he was
up and off for the woods. How pure and free
seemed the fresh air of heaven! God speed and
shield the flying boy! At the next station, the
guard of the train gave the alarm, and soon a
pack of five blood-hounds, with their mounted
brutal keepers, were on his track, and in full
pursuit. Bravely but vainly Manning sought to
retain the freedom he had won at such fearful
risk. Plunging into the recesses of a dismal
swamp, he had brief hope that he should evade
his pursuers; but soon the baying of the hounds
was in his strained ears, and about him were the
ringing echoes of the on-spurring guard. His
hiding-place was speedily surrounded, and his
hope of escape cut off. Yet he clung to dear
liberty to the last. Again and again came the
blaspheming shouts of his pursuers, demanding
his surrender, and threatening him with "no
quarter" if he compelled them to push further
through the entangling briers and slimy morasses.

He waded out into the sluggish waters of the inner swamp depths, to turn if possible the trail of the keen-scented hounds; but with undeviating directness they bounded towards him through brake and fen: he heard their labored breathing; then caught a glimpse of their flashing eyes and foaming jaws, as, with a vindictive howl at their long-delayed triumph, they leaped ferociously out of the thicket into the water where he stood, firm in despair. "Oh! 'twas a horrid moment," he said, " when they caught me and made a spring for my throat. I sank in the mire: a gurgling sound filled my ears —" One hound clutched him by the shoulder as he fell in the water: another sent his sharp fangs through the flesh of his side. As he rolled in the deadly struggle, the keepers came up and choked off the dogs, although one of them was urgent to have him torn in pieces because of his temerity. Weak, bruised, bleeding, despondent, Manning was carried to the Andersonville stockade, there to have his only nursing at the hands of the keepers of that accursed den, amid its exposures, its privations, its gloom, and its loathsomeness.

ANDERSONVILLE HORRORS.

Oh, how wearily the hours dragged in Andersonville! Shivering, unsheltered, in the cold nights of rain; sweltering, all exposed, under the noonday's sun; cramped in the seething mass of the close-packed stockade, where half-naked men strove with each other for the last garment from the body of their latest dead comrade; weighed down with the poison-laden air of the malarial swamp; knowing no relief from the gnawings of hunger in the soul-straining processes of slow starvation; needing Christian courage to hold back from the relief of the dead-line; full of sad forebodings of evil to home loved ones who mourned him as dead, and from whom no comforting word could come; and chafing, most of all, in his overwrought and high-strung nervous powers, under enforced inaction at a time when every patriot's strength should tell for God and Government, — Manning's life wasted surely away, and his system imbibed fairly that disease which at length destroyed his firm and vigorous constitution, and brought him so early in life's day to the house appointed to all living.

IN THE REBEL RANKS. — LOYAL STILL.

Finding himself still held as a suspected spy, although the special charges against him had been lost, and denied the treatment of an ordinary prisoner of war, Manning prayerfully deter mined on a course he would not have counselled for one captured in open battle. The special orders from his department commander clearly authorized such a proceeding in his case, and he sought to find a temporary place in the rebel ranks, that he might escape to the Union lines with the valuable information he had in various ways obtained. Circumstances providentially favored him, and he adroitly managed to pass out with a squad who had regularly enlisted; and, without taking any oath of allegiance to the "Confederate" powers, he was counted and equipped as a soldier in that army, and hurried towards the rebel front. However any might question the propriety or policy of this move-ment on his part, it cannot be denied that in it he acted conscientiously, and verily felt he was doing God service. He was acting for his government, to which he was loyal as ever, and was carrying out the very letter and spirit of his specific instructions. "I gained all the information I could, from every thing that passed," he wrote, "and laid it up in my memory. When I saw a big bridge, I studied how I might blow it up; when I passed a large city, I was planning how I might set it on fire; and when I saw a leading general, I was contriving some way how I might blow his brains out. I was in the enemy's country, — nothing but enemies around me; and the more harm I could do them, the greater service I should be doing my country." It was not long before the Union cavalry made a dash on the rebel lines in Manning's vicinity. At once he ran for the battle-line of the assailing force, facing its sharpest fire, while also fired at by his rebel comrades who divined the object of his move; and he reached the Union ranks unharmed.

A PRISONER AMONG FRIENDS.—GOOD NEWS FOR HOME.

Once more under the old flag, Manning told his strange story to the commander before whom he was taken ; but it is not to be wondered at that it was discredited, in the absence of proof. He was deemed a rebel prisoner, and as such was sent to the military prison at Alton, Illinois. Sending forward his complaint to his regiment, he was, after a few weeks' delay, ordered released by direct command from the War Department. It was then — for he would not write to his dear ones while a prisoner at Alton — that he sent his first letter home. The simple message, —

"St. Louis, Mo. March 10, 1865.

"My dear Loved' Ones, —
  "I still live, and you shall hear from me soon.
"Henry H. Manning."

written on a sheet of "Christian Commission" paper, with the appropriate printed motto, "Let it hasten to those who wait for tidings," — came as a voice from the grave to those who had mourned him, and gave to them glad and grateful hearts; for now their dead was alive again, and their lost was found.

AGAIN WITH HIS REGIMENT.—MERITED PROMOTION.

Subjected, on his way to his regiment, to those vexatious arrests and detentions to which an enlisted man absent from his command without a " descriptive list" was liable, in war time, Manning at length rejoined his comrades of the Twenty-fourth, at Richmond, Va., where the regiment was doing provost duty, about the middle of April, 1865. The ten months intervening since he left his command, not a dozen miles from where he now rejoined it, had been teeming ones to the gallant and war-worn battalion in its varied campaigning, as well as to himself within the enemy's lines. He missed many a comrade who had fallen in the fight while he suffered in the hands of the foe. But they were hearty greetings that passed between those who at last. thus met in safety and dear-bought peace.

The following regimental order shows something of the estimate put on his services by his immediate commander : —

> HEADQUARTERS 24th Mass. Vol. Inf.
> RICHMOND, VA., April 22, 1865.

SPECIAL ORDER NO. 34.

Corporal H. H. Manning, Co. G, is hereby promoted to be sergeant in the same company, as a special commendation for the services rendered by him.

Captured within the lines of the enemy while on secret service, and arraigned for trial as a spy. Sergeant Manning passed through a series of dangerous adventures, sufficient to shake the firmest resolution. Throughout his captivity he displayed a courage and constancy to duty which deserve a greater reward than his commanding officer has power to bestow.

> By order of
> ALBERT ORDWAY,
> Lieut.-Col. 24th Mass. Vol. Inf. Comd'g Regt.

BENJ. F. STODDARD,
　1st Lieut. and Adj.

HOME AT LAST.

Manning was too far reduced by his prison life to be of further use in the army; moreover, active campaigning was at an end; and he was honorably discharged, June 16, 1865, after nearly four years of such service as few even of the Union soldiers in the late war were called to.

Returning to his Massachusetts home, his first
effort was to rebuild his health. A visit to the
West refreshed him, and he hoped for ultimate
recovery. Investing his army earnings for the
benefit of his home loved ones, he looked about
him for something to do. He had not forgotten
his promise to God. in Macon jail : his only
doubt was how he could best redeem it.

TELLING HIS STORY. — FULFILLING HIS VOW.

Visiting an army comrade in North Bridgewater, Manning met the Rev. S. H. Lee, now
of Greenfield, who counselled him to attempt
studying for the ministry ; and, that he might
procure funds to start with, Mr. Lee suggested
his preparing a lecture on his army service and
prison adventures, to deliver as opportunity of-
fered, until the proceeds of it should amount to one
hundred dollars, when he could hopefully com-
mence school-life, and thenceforward work his
way along through a course of study. The lecture was prepared, and, under Mr. Lee's aus-
pices, brought out at North Bridgewater. It

was repeated a score of times or so, during the winter of 1865-6, with good success. It is much to be regretted that no copy of this manuscript was retained; for Manning wrote with no little graphic power, and such a record of his eventful soldier-life would have proved of thrilling interest now.

STUDENT-LIFE AT ANDOVER. — LOVING SERVICE FOR JESUS.

In the spring of 1866, he was on his way to Phillips Academy, Andover, with the one hundred dollars in hand, — or rather with one hundred and one dollars; and, as he had been advised to start with one hundred, he gave the odd dollar to a poor man on the road. At Andover, while an earnest student, he was an untiring Christian worker. He taught in a mission-school, took part in prayer-meetings, and conversed on the subject of personal religion with many school-mates, winning thus friends to himself and souls to Jesus. His life really seemed — as he had promised it should be — wholly consecrate to Jesus. " Way down

in the inmost recesses of my heart," he wrote,
" the great all-absorbing purpose and desire is to
do the will of God as it is made known to me by
his providence. . . . I desire to be led by the
hand of God. . . . I wish to do away with
every selfish thought, and live only for Jesus."
Yet he worked from no mere sense of stern duty,
in the slavish performance of a binding vow :
love prompted his service, out of a willing heart.
" How much real enjoyment it gives me to work
for Jesus!" he said. " All other pleasures fade
away and are lost, by the side of it." And this
enjoyment in work for Jesus was increased by
the conviction that souls were benefited by it.
He loved to work for others, because Jesus com-
manded it ; and he loved to work for Jesus, because others were blessed by it. " You know,"
he said, " the words of our Saviour are, ' Inas-
much as ye have done it unto one of the least of
these my brethren, ye have done it unto me.'
How soothing and encouraging these words are !
I don't see how any one can help doing all the
good they can. . . . I have an insatiable thirst
after perishing souls, and hope and pray that

God will lead me to do good wherever I am.
. . . I am thankful for the hope that, perhaps ·
ere long, I can throw aside all other things,
and enter with my whole heart upon the work
of saving souls. . . . . My heart pants to be
wholly engaged in my Master's service."

TOIL FOR BREAD. — ÜNFAILING TRUST.

One hundred dollars will not go far towards a
young man's thorough education, nowadays;
and Manning found himself before long pressed
for means of support. Then he was driven to
work hard for money, while toiling incessantly
at study. He swept the school-rooms, and performed similar service at the academy, for fifteen
cents an hour; he went out in the early morn-
ings to do mowing and other farm labor, until
the hour of school-time; and thus he kept along
in every thing but health and rest. He had no
odd hours unimproved. Writing of his mission-
scholars, in whom he was deeply interested, he
said, " I generally spend two evenings a week
with them, and two evenings at literary societies
for improvement of the mind, and there are not

often but three evenings left, and those are our prayer-meeting nights."

Had Manning been in full health, he might have stood all this; but disease, fastened on him in the prison stockade, never relaxed its hold; and his strength failed steadily. Some of his friends advised him to abandon student-life and seek renewed vigor in active out-door occupation; but others, who were nearest him, with unaccountable blindness and persistency, uniformly urged his adherence to first-formed plans. Again and again his enfeebled frame gave way; and as often his unwavering determination enabled him to rally for another effort. It was hard for him to relinquish his purpose of *activity* in Christ's service. He was far from wilful in this struggle. "I desire to be led by the hand of God," he said ; "I am praying very earnestly, . . . asking God to tell me what to do, and I know he will not tell me wrong. . . . Feeling that I am performing my mission here on earth, I take every step gladly ;" but he wanted to take some step, not to stand still : it was easier for him to do any thing for Christ than to do nothing. "I will endeavor," he wrote, "to keep within bounds, and not try to strain my rope when I find I have arrived at the end of it;" but he was loath to believe there was any end to his rope. "God willing, I shall be able to do something by and by," he said, "and what shall it be?" He had the feeling that God, having accepted his consecration vow in prison, would somehow find work for him to do for Jesus, in accordance with its terms. No lesson concerning God's "kingly state" seemed so hard for him to learn as that —

"They also serve who only stand and wait."

And, doubtless, his energy, coupled with his faith, prolonged his useful life. In his condition, and with his temperament, he would have fallen sooner but for his indomitable will, his determination not yet to yield to the closing pressure of disease, and his conviction that God would still sustain him in his work; that so long as he did what he could and should, his Father would supply all lack. It is, unquestionably, every man's duty to consider his health, even in the prosecution of a religious enterprise, and no

desire for high and holy attainment will justify
reckless over-effort of body or mind. But not
all are to be judged by the same standard of
prudence in amount or kinds of effort or toil.
What is rest for one man would prove torture
to another. Not a few depend for very life upon
tireless activity; like the traveller on the Alps,
if in their exhaustion they sit down at the ap-
proach of night, they chill and sleep and die.
They must keep moving or perish. So in the
case of Henry Manning: while his example of
unintermitted nervous endeavor may not be com-
mended to ordinary men for imitation, it may be
admired and approved in him, doomed as he
was to an early death from the hour he entered
the Petersburg dungeon, and kept alive through ·
his resolute activity, his over-estimate of remain-
ing strength, and his ever sanguine anticipations
of returning health.

And with all his weakness of body, his faith
never faltered. "If God wants me to stay
at school," he said while at Andover, " I have
no fear but that he will find a way for me to get
along there." Then he told of his rising one

morning without a cent of money in the world, and going earnestly to God in prayer for help, and of his finding, but a few minutes later, between the pages of the book he took up to study, fifteen dollars (which God had put it into the heart of some friend to give to him in that delicate way) ; and he added, in affirmation of his undoubting faith, " And God will do so again if it is best."

FAILING HEALTH. — A GRATEFUL HEART.

It was in the spring of 1867, that Manning finally left his studies. He struggled manfully with disease, but it gained on him steadily. He visited among friends, to try change of air and scene, and was under various medical treatment, but all to little purpose. His prison privations were working out in his shattered constitution their inevitable result. For all attention shown or aid rendered him, he was ever grateful, and he seemed to feel that none had better friends than he. Of a pleasant home where he had passed a brief time, he wrote, " It's a second paradise : isn't it? If Christ was on earth now,

I do believe that he would make his home there
— a part of the time at least: don't you?"

Those who were privileged to assist him from
time to time may surely feel, as he felt, that their
gifts were unto the Lord. " I want assistance,"
he wrote on this point, once, " only that I may
be useful ; and, strictly speaking, I want to be
useful only for Jesus !" To God he gave glory
for whatever help came to him from any direc-
tion. Returning thanks for a generous donation
—which proved most timely — from one who
sent it as " a cup of cold water to a disciple,"
he said, feelingly, " How very strange and
mysterious are the Lord's dealings with this
poor weak child of his ! Every earthly prop is
struck from under me, and I am just sinking in
utter hopeless despair, when the Lord not only
succors and relieves me, but catches me right
up in his arms, and gives me such blessings as
I had no thought of asking for."

IN HOSPITAL. — GENTLE MINISTRY THERE.

In his health-seeking, Manning visited Boston
to secure the valued counsel of Dr. S. A. Green,

his former regimental surgeon, who had on many occasions shown special interest in him, and expressed a readiness to aid him to the utmost. Soon there came a letter from him, dated in the Massachusetts General Hospital, saying, " My health has been growing frailer of late, and yesterday I came to this city, hoping to see Dr. Green, and perhaps get into some hospital; but on arriving here I found that Dr. G. was in Europe! . . . So, with an earnest prayer on my lips, I turned back, and, after much difficulty, found my way to this place, — found the head of the institution, and told my story — simple and short! Out of health, out of money, and disappointed about meeting friends.

" Well, I was told that this was just the place for folks in such a condition, and I was hustled into a warm bath, and into Ward 23, among a set of ghastly, half-in-the-grave looking fellows, some of whom lay, or sat up, in bed, like marble posts; some were cracking vulgar jokes, and one or two of the most deathly-looking ones were cursing and grumbling because they could not be allowed a pint of whiskey a day. . . . Perhaps I am wrong,

but I can't help feeling grieved, mortified, and
sad to come here so like a beggar! but what
could I do? Here I've been on expense, more or
less, ever since I left school, and no way of getting
money. I have parted with my watch, and expect
to receive ten or fifteen dollars for that shortly ; so
I shall get on nicely, only it galls me to have to be
in this situation here! but I hope I shall not be
here long. .... And if I can get my health again,
I shall know how to prize it; and shall be as
thankful to God as I was when released from
prison."

He was as unselfish in. hospital as elsewhere.
Having a little money left with him by friends,
for the purchase of such comforts as he might
crave, he at once set about ministering to the
needs of those about him in the different wards,
finding it ever " more blessed to give than to receive."

" Perhaps it may be gratifying to you," he
wrote, in returning thanks for kindness shown
to him by a slight gift, " to know of some of the
effects of that kindness ; of some of the good it
has brought about, and some of the hearts it has

cheered. That poor, deformed, ghastly-looking
boy that I pointed out to you while we were
conversing together in the hospital, wanted many
things that were not furnished him. I expended
a little of that money that you left with me upon
him, . . . and it would send a thrill of pleasure
through and through you to have noted the effect.
He was so unused to kindness that it quite over-
came him. Poor, dear fellow! He is not long
for this world. May the Lord watch over him,
and prepare him for the future!

"And then there was a poor Irish girl in one of
the wards, a Catholic, but one of the most de-
voted Christian girls I ever met. . . . Her home
is in Ireland; but while visiting in this country,
she met with a fearful accident, and was sent
to the hospital for treatment. When I met her
she was recovering, but was feeling somewhat
disheartened because her friends were so far
away; and she was often slighted on account of
her being an 'Irish Catholic.' . . . I was enabled to cheer her up a great deal, and to do one
or two little substantial acts of kindness for her,
which went directly to her heart, and seemed to

do her so much good that I thanked God, invol-
untarily, for the opportunity of cheering her, and
being of service to her.

" But I was enabled to render the most assistance to an American lady, — a noble-hearted
woman and a true Christian. Her life has
been one of adventure and suffering, and one
cannot listen to the recital of her touching story
without feeling deeply interested in her. She
has been in the hospital a long time, and is
at present very weak and frail; and there is a
great deal of doubt about her ever being any
better. I bought little things for her that I knew
did her good; and when I came away I left a
very little money with her, in order that she
might be able to procure any little thing that
she felt as if she couldn't do without, even if
the hospital did not furnish it. And so I had
the pleasure of leaving her quite light-hearted
and hopeful, believing more firmly than ever that
the Lord would care for her, and never, never
forsake her."

. It was indeed a privilege to give assistance in
any way to one so grateful as was Manning, for

all that he received of blessing, and so ready to make others happy by ministering discreetly, and in a loving, Christ-like spirit, to the needy and heavy-burdened about him.

HOPE AGAINST HOPE.—THE PRIVILEGE OF CHRISTIAN WORK.

From the hospital to his home, and again among friends who felt that his presence with them was in itself a blessing, Manning still sought health, while growing gradually weaker and less able to exert himself in body or mind. He would not see the dark side of his case, but still confidently hoped for recovery. " I don't feel natural yet, by any means," he wrote from Fisk-dale, where he was with good friends on a farm, in October, 1867, " nor free from mental weakness, but I'm stronger physically than I have been since I left Andover, certain. You see we are a mile and a half from neighbors, and my friends are very quiet indeed, so I talk hardly any ; and when I get to work husking corn, digging potatoes, and the like, I often even forget to *think*, and I gain by it rapidly ; but

when I come down to writing letters, it puts me
back."

Manning's days of struggle with disease were
not wholly profitless to others. He was the
means of not a little good, in his moving from
point to point in the last year of his toilsome
life. At South Danvers, Bridgewater, Fiskdale,
Winchester, Beverly, Hartford, and elsewhere,
he raised his voice or used his warm and loving
heart for precious souls, in ways that will never
be forgotten. His crown in heaven will be bright
with stars won in those months of vain search
for health. And this work was ever a joy to
him, and he thanked God for his part in it.

While in the hospital at Boston, he told in sad-
ness of his disappointments in efforts at Christian
activity, — of his going to a place in Vermont
where was such need of religious endeavor that
" even he could do something for Jesus," and of
his being taken ill on the very day of his arrival
there, and thus prevented raising his voice for the
Master. " And so it has often been," he added,
regretfully. " I don't know whether I've learned
the right lesson from all this ; but this is what it

seems to me God is teaching me by these disappointments: It is a blessed privilege to work for Jesus. Jesus didn't need me in Vermont. He has never needed me anywhere; but he has let me work for him sometimes. Oh, if I ever get well enough to work for him again, won't I be thankful for it!" Would to God that all Christians had learned this lesson as well!

ONLY WAITING.—REST AT LAST.

At length the prolonged struggle drew towards its close. Early in May last, Manning — told by the physicians in a water-cure establishment, where he had been spending some months, that nothing more could be done for him with hope — turned his steps for the last time to his Warwick home. He still had hope of recovery, for he had passed so many perils safely that he could hardly realize there was any death for him; but he was now more resigned to inaction, in the same trustful love of Jesus and his cause. "I know that my Saviour will take care of me," he wrote: "I don't *think* it, I *know* it! I haven't the slightest doubt of it. He never manifested

himself to me more wonderfully than he has of
late; never satisfied the cravings of my heart
more, or filled my soul more full! And I believe I never had so much love for him, or loved
to speak of him to others, so well, as at the present time!" But he added, "It is not my busi-
ness to think whether I am to live or die, but,
rather, how I can best serve Christ. I want to
do any thing, and be any thing, and suffer any
thing that he wants me to." So, as he lay down
on his home-bed to die, he had learned his last
lesson, — he could wait as well as work.

> " He was not eager, bold,
>   Nor strong, — all that was past;
> He was ready not to do,
>   At last, at last."

His faith grew firmer as his flesh failed, and
the less he could himself do, the more he was
ready to trust God to do for him. On one occasion, when it seemed as if his hour of death had
come, his sisters who were nearest were all sum-
moned to his bedside, and just then two other
sisters came in unexpectedly, — one from Boston,
the other from Wisconsin, — while a friend whom

he had particularly desired to see again, also
visited him. For the first time in several years
the family were all together at home. This
moved Manning to profoundest gratitude to God,
and he repeatedly referred to it in this spirit, tell-
ing over the story of recent blessings secured to
himself and his loved ones, as though he had
just pride in the power and goodness of his
heavenly Father, who had done all this for his
comfort. Again, when he was pressed for means
to supply his daily necessities, a sister came to
him one morning to say that a letter had been received covering a gift of thirty dollars for his use.
A pleasant smile came over his face as he re-
sponded, " I prayed for money last night. It
was the first time I had asked for that in a good
while."

There were long and weary weeks for him of
final trial in racking pain — the whole inner system destroyed by the foul air of swamp and dungeon, and the scant or vile food of stockade and
jail, while the still young and naturally vigorous
outer man refused to be yet wholly crushed.
There were dreams of prison-life, hunger and

thirst ever unsatisfied; and seasons of agony in
struggle for breath, as with slow, wasting flesh,
and cold, clammy brow, the patient sufferer
whispered with livid lips, in unfailing trust, " I
want nothing; I wish for nothing; I hope for
nothing: I only wait," until death brought relief
and rest on the evening of Friday, Sept. 4, 1868.
Two days later, his remains were borne out by
loving hands from the church where, seven years
before, that very month, he had stood up to wit-
ness for Jesus before going out to face death at
the call of God, and tenderly laid away under
the green turf of the neighboring hill-side ceme-
tery, close by the tasteful granite shaft which
stands " In Memory of Warwick's Soldiers who
fell in the War of the Great Rebellion."

CLAIMS OF THE DEAD ON THE LIVING.

And thus the earthly warfare of another brave
soldier is concluded. His was a noble work, — a
work for others; for his fellows, his country, his
God. " Greater love hath no man than this,
that a man lay down his life for his friends."
Henry Manning " hath done what he could " for

the interests dear to the hearts of the Union sol-
.diers. It is for those who survive him to hold
sacred, and to guard jealously the principles and
privileges — the supremacy of the Federal Government; the integrity of the national Union ;
the just liberties of the people of the Republic ;
the protection in their every right of all its citi-
·zens; the execution of the laws, and the inviola-
bility of the national faith — for which he and so
many other soldiers battled, endured, and prayed,
and gave or risked their lives.

And the faith of Henry Manning should be
deemed yet more admirable and holy than his
work. His work was heroic : his. faith was
sublime! It was because of his faith in that
Saviour who died for him, and was an ever-pres-
ent help in all his needs, that he went out as a
soldier, and endured unto the end so bravely.
" He fought a good fight" because he " kept the
faith." " Through faith " he " escaped the edge
of the sword ; out of weakness was made strong,
waxed valiant in fight," " had trial . . . of bonds
and imprisonment, . . . being destitute, afflicted,
tormented," and out of all " obtained a good re-

port ; " and finally has " gotten the victory," and received "a crown of glory that fadeth not away."

Surely in view of his faith and his faithfulness, and of the cause for which Henry Manning lived and gave his life, it behooves the lovers of their Country and of the Cross, to " hold such in reputation, because, for the sake of Christ, he was nigh unto death, not regarding his life to supply their lack of service."

Cambridge : Press of John Wilson and Son.